10 0692155 6

UNIVER...GHAM
WITHDRAWN
FROM THE LIBRARY

D0533640

Picture Credits:
All pictures by Pete

Fig 5.23, Fig 5.24, Fig... Fig 5.33,
Fig 5.34, Fig 5.35, Fig... 5.37, Fig 5.38
Copyright of The Angle Ring Company Ltd.

Fabrication - The Designers Guide

Instead of imposing a cerebral form on an inert matter, materials were allowed to have their say in the final form produced. Craftsmen did not impose a shape but rather teased out a form from a material, acting more as triggers for spontaneous behaviour than as commanders imposing their desires from above. In all this there was a respect for matter's form-generating capabilities and an ability to deal with heterogeneity.

Manuel De Landa, Philosophies of Design

Fabrication - The Designers Guide

Fabrication - The Designers Guide
the illustrated works of twelve
specialist UK fabricators

researched and written
Pete Silver, William McLean,
Simon Veglio

edited
Samantha Hardingham

photography
Pete Silver, William McLean
except where indicated

University of Nottingham
Hallward Library

GEORGE GREEN LIBRARY OF
SCIENCE AND ENGINEERING

Routledge
Taylor & Francis Group

LONDON AND NEW YORK

Architectural Press is an imprint of Routledge
2 Park Square, Milton Park, Oxon, OX14 4RN
711 Third Avenue, New York, NY 10017

Routledge is an imprint of the Taylor & Francis Group, an informa business

First Edition 2006

Copyright © 2006 Pete Silver, William McLean, Samantha Hardingham, Simon Veglio. All rights reserved

No part of this publication may be reproduced in any material form (including photocopying or storing in any medium by electronic means and whether or not transiently or incidentally to some other use of this publication) without the written permission of the copyright holder except in accordance with the provisions of the Copyright, Designs and Patents Act 1988 or under the terms of a licence issued by the Copyright Licensing Agency Ltd, 90 Tottenham Court Road, London, England W1T 4LP. Applications for the copyright holder's written permission to reproduce any part of this publication should be addressed to the publisher

British Library Cataloguing in Publication Data
A catalogue record for this book is available from the British Library

Library of Congress Cataloguing in Publication Data
A catalogue record for this book is available from the Library of Congress

ISBN 0 7506 6558 0

1006921556

Contents

Dr Johnson said that a lack of manual dexterity constitutes a form of ignorance.

Writer Will Self

Authors' note
Most fabrication processes involve a series of primary actions such as cutting, sawing, bending or welding, with the precise nature of the process determined by the raw elements and materials to which they are applied. This book is divided into sections, each of which is dedicated to the actions of particular fabricators as applied to specific primary materials.

In all cases, the ability to move raw materials and finished products around factories, building sites, and indeed around the world, places finite limitations on the size, shape and weight of prefabricated objects. Fabricators also optimise their use of materials, utilising computer software to minimise wastage in sheet stock such as glass and steel and aluminium.

Foreword

Since time immemorial man has been using materials to craft his buildings, his tools and the objects of every day life. Over the last twenty years the rise of information technology has changed the way we conceptualise and design the objects around us, and yet paradoxically with this ever increasing power to visualise ideas we are in danger of distancing ourselves from the physical limitations and opportunities presented to us by the materials we use, and the processes by which these materials are transformed.

This book examines a diverse and eclectic range of different technologies, ranging on the one hand from the ancient craft skills of moulding ductile iron or sitka spruce, skills which have evolved over generations, to processes where materials can in effect be designed to order.

The underlying theme common throughout the book is that design, fabrication, and material properties are integrally linked. The fabrication process is defined not only by the end goal that a client requires but more critically by the industries, processes and technologies that have developed out of a profound understanding of the how a material works, what it is good at, and what it likes.

As such this book forms an invaluable tool for the designer to more fully understand the properties of the materials and their transformation into useful objects in our lives through human intervention.

Furthermore I hope very much that this book will not only assist designers in understanding the materials of their craft, and assist in the adaptation of their ideas to suit the fabrication processes involved but also to allow them to celebrate the fabrication process as part of the language of design itself.

Ben Morris
Vector Foiltec

The Vector Foiltec group was established in 1981 by Ben Morris in London and Dr Stefan Lehnert in Germany. The group specializes in the design and construction of ETFE (Ethylene Tetraflouroethylene) cushion structures and lightweight kinetic enclosures. Vector Foiltec are currently working on roofing Beijing's 2008 Olympic stadium.

Introduction

Tools

When trying to characterise the human species in the context of evolution, most scientists adopt a simple criteria - though not exclusive to humans, what distinguishes humans from other species is their use of tools.

This book documents the work of a group of specialist fabricators currently operating in the UK, their work ranging from the manufacture of complex wire rope to timber masts and spars, from large-scale composite casting to computer controlled, sheet steel fabrication. Each process is described through a photographic tour of the tools, techniques and activities employed in transforming formless or primary materials into products.

Design

In the early 1960s, American oceanographers designed an advanced submersible in order to carry out much needed underwater research. The fully manoeuvrable mini-submarine was to be funded by the US Navy, but for various reasons the designers couldn't find anyone willing to build it. Eventually, Alvin, as it was named, was constructed by General Mills, the food company, at a factory where it made the machines to produce breakfast cereals.

This is not untypical of the fabrication industry. While many of our specialist fabricators do manufacture standardised components, the majority make bespoke products to order; they produce one-off items or limited production runs, and clients will come from a variety of backgrounds and disciplines. For each product, the designer must be able to clearly communicate his ideas, and the fabricator must be able to relate those ideas to his specialist processes. At times, fabricators will adapt their process to suit the product - this may involve 'tinkering' with a multi-million pound tool. Similarly designers may have to adapt their ideas to suit the limitations of the fabrication processes. The more symbiotic this relationship, the more cost-effective the process and the more satisfactory the product.

It is hoped that this book can improve the designer's understanding and appreciation of some of the most common fabrication processes.

Experience

While our UK fabricators are not quite as successful as their ancient counterparts in Kenya, who are said to have manufactured axe-heads over a period of roughly a million years, many have nonetheless been manufacturing products over a number of generations. It is this accumulated knowledge that enables them to adapt successfully to new demands and challenges. Fabricators conduct their own research. John Dent Engineering make a range of finely tailored exhaust pipes for prototyping on racing motorcycles, and Collars of Oxford make some of the longest timber yacht masts commercially available. Some fabricators are exploring the limits of new materials (such as Kevlar-cored ropes) while others are developing new techniques for traditional materials (like computer-controlled stone cutting).

While tools are becoming more sophisticated and many products are now manufactured with little or no 'hands on' human intervention, aspects of craft and technique are still present in most fabrication processes. It is often only the direct interaction of humans and materials that can create a unique object. This book functions to promote exemplary practice and human endeavour. It is time dependent and as such will subsequently become a document of record, albeit a small sample, of current manufacturing and fabrication in the UK.

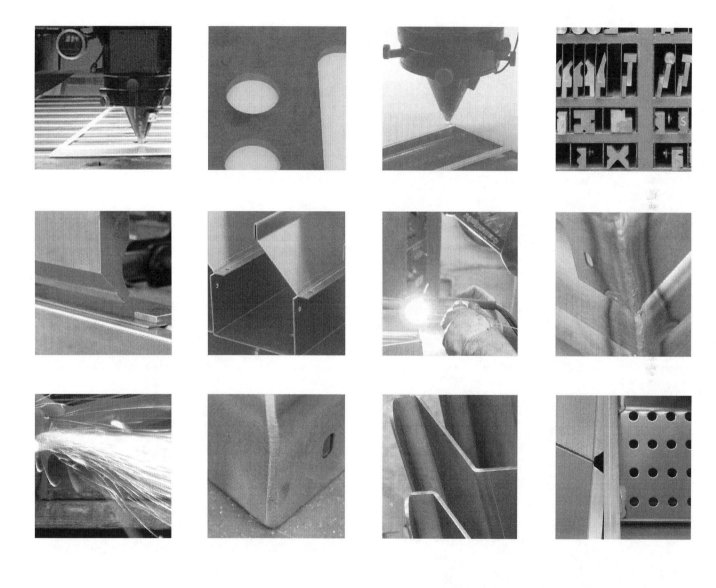

Sheet Metal

Fig 1.0 Sheet metal

Sheet Metal
John Dent Engineering, Isleworth

Sheet Materials
Sheet materials come in various types, from mild steels to timber and plastics, and with varying degrees of thickness. If designers need sheet materials to be cut to size with precision, or if multiples are required, specialist fabricators provide the tools and expertise necessary for their production. Such fabricators will also have machines for folding sheet metal into complex shapes and will be able to finish (weld, polish, paint) products in a variety of ways.

Laser Cutting
CNC (Computer Numerically Controlled) laser cutting is a process in which a shape is cut from sheet material using an intense laser beam that cuts

Fig 1.1 Metal sections

Fig 1.2 CNC laser

Fig 1.3 CNC cutting bench

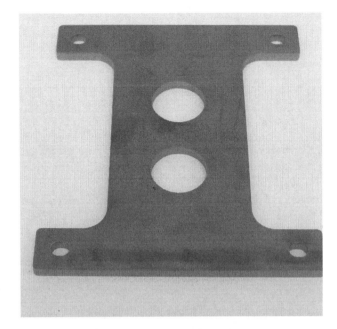

Fig 1.4 CNC Laser-cut, 8mm sheet steel

by melting the material in the beam path. The process is particularly cost-effective for prototyping and short runs, since no physical tooling is needed and the process can accept almost any geometric shape. Lasers have interchangeable optics for different materials and depths of cut. Lasers work best on materials such as carbon steel - an alloy of iron and carbon (2%) or stainless steel - a corrosion resistant alloy of steel and chromium (10.5%). Metals such as aluminium and copper alloys are more difficult (slower) to cut by laser due to their ability to reflect the laser light as well as absorb and conduct heat - these materials require more powerful lasers.

A laser can cut through a 1m long, 10mm thick, steel panel in around 30 seconds, but the thicker the steel the larger the curve that will form when cutting around corners. CNC lasers are housed in

Fig 1.5 CNC laser-cut, 10mm sheet steel

Fig 1.6 CNC laser cutting 5mm plastic sheet

Fig 1.7 John Dent Engineering

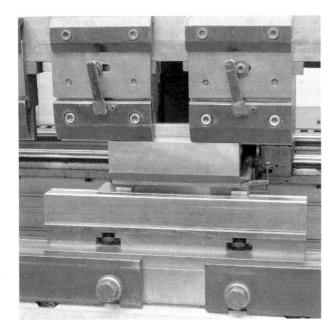

Fig 1.8 Press brake tool head

x/y/z-axis gantries that can be programmed to cut from CAD drawings like a large plotter. They are accurate to within 50 microns and parts remain flat.

Maximum material cutting capacities are:
Mild steel - 12mm
Stainless steel (clean cut) - 3mm
Stainless steel (oxygen cut) - 12mm
Aluminium - 4mm
Brass - 2.5mm
Woods and Plastics - 30mm
Maximum sheet size - 3000mm x 1270mm
Maximum weight - 250kg

Folding and Finishing
Once they have been cut into shape, malleable materials (i.e. those like sheet metal that can be folded without loss of structural integrity) can be formed into complex, three-dimensional shapes by

Fig 1.9 Tool head showing fold profile

Fig 1.10 Tooling library

Fig 1.11 Eight-axis, full CNC press brake

Fig 1.12 Sheet metal, cut and folded

multi-axis folding machine. An 80 tonne press brake can fold sheet metal up to 10mm thick.

Folding

Sheets are folded by being compressed over interchangeable tool heads, and fabricators will make use of extensive tooling libraries to construct multi-tool set-ups for each product. CNC machines can be programmed to carry out folding procedures of up to eight axes, and, according to the thickness of the material, programmes help calculate the tolerances to be made for the natural curvatures formed along the edges.

Once folded into shape, products are assembled and finished by hand. They may be welded, riveted or bolted together and can then be subjected to a variety of surface treatments such as plating, engraving or silk-screening.

Fig 1.13 Sheet metal, cut and folded

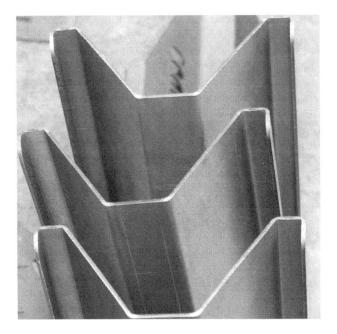

Fig 1.14 Hand finished folded sheet metal profiles

Fig 1.15 Stainless steel containers ready for finishing

Fig 1.16 Welding sheet metal

The Machines
Laser cutting:
Amada LC-1212 Alpha II, 2D, 1.5kW CO_2 cross flow oscillator, full CNC

Folding:
Amada 50-20 HFB, 2.0 metre, 50 ton, 8 axis, full CNC
Amada 80-25 APX, 2.5 metre, 80 ton, 8 axis, full CNC
Promecam 25-12, 1.2 metre, 25 ton

All machines are computer numerically controlled and graphics software can be used as a source for their instructions. CAD files are exported as DXF files, and CAD/CAM software is used to create the codes that are used for directing the machines.

Fig 1.17 Finished corner welds

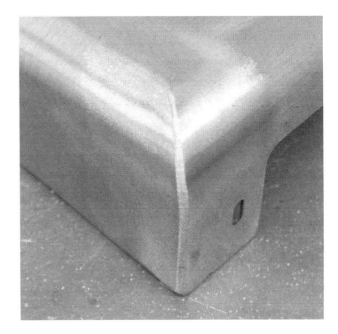

Fig 1.18 Welded corners ground to a finish

Fig 1.19 Grinding with a rotary, abrasive wheel

Fig 1.20 Assembly detail

The Fabricator
John Dent Engineering was formed in 1976, specialising in precision sheet metal work. The family firm now employs state-of-the-art CNC machinery as well as a highly trained and skilled workforce. The company won a major award at the 1992 Precision Sheet Metal Fair in Japan, and now serves an array of industries, developing prototypes and undertaking a wide range of batch runs.

Fig 1.21 Finished bracket product with punched holes

Fig 1.22 Finished air filter product

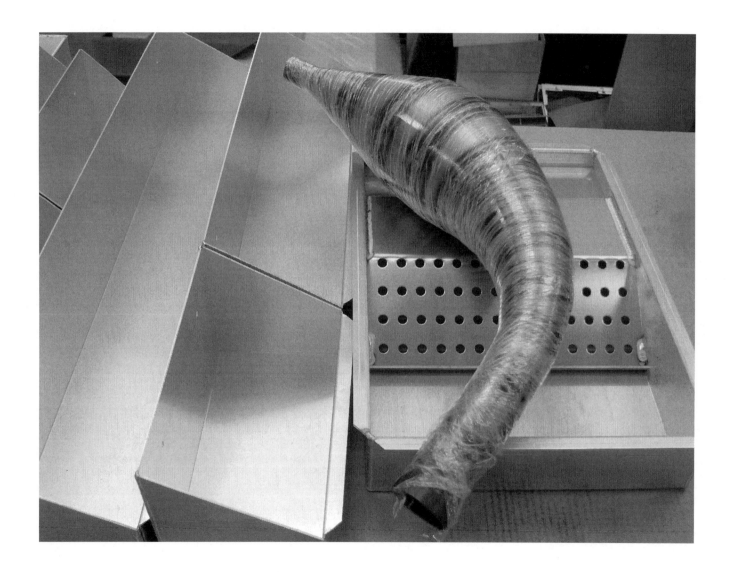

Fig 1.23 Examples of finished products

2

Softwood Timber

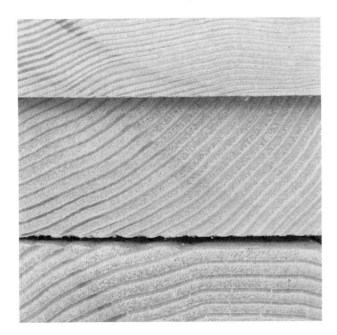

Fig 2.0 Alaskan Sitka spruce

Softwood Timber
Collars, Oxford

Sitka Spruce
The fabrication of a long, straight timber mast depends in the first instance upon the quality of the raw material and the way in which it is treated. Yacht masts and rowing oars are made from Alaskan Sitka spruce, also known as 'aviation quality spruce'. Chosen for its size, growth rate and purity (lack of knots) this timber softwood is kiln dried in order to remove excess moisture and to relieve tension in the wood.

Every timber mast or rowing oar begins its life as a design drawing which is then translated into three-dimensional form through the acts of cutting and carving into an organic material. Every piece of wood has its own unique 'fingerprint' and the

Fig 2.1 Organic waste

Fig 2.2 Plank has been hollowed out by routing

Fig 2.3 Straight and 'true'

Fig 2.4 Detail of laminated mast

craftsman must act upon it accordingly. Wood is chosen on the basis of having an even balance of stresses within the plank. If a tree has grown on the side of a hill it will grow stronger on one side and the stresses will be locked in to create a harder 'red' wood that will eventually cause a plank to warp - to twist or bow.

A rough sawn Sitka spruce plank will arrive at the joiner's workshop just as it left the logging mill. It will then go through a number of processes prior to final shaping. In a typical hollow mast, the plank will be split along its length using a bench saw and then machine planed. The plank will then be hollowed or routed for lightness before being rejoined with its other half (known as laminating) prior to shaping. All of these processes are accurately timed and monitored so that the timber maintains its balance and straightness throughout the operation.

Fig 2.5 Scarf connecting joint

Fig 2.6 Shaping work in progress

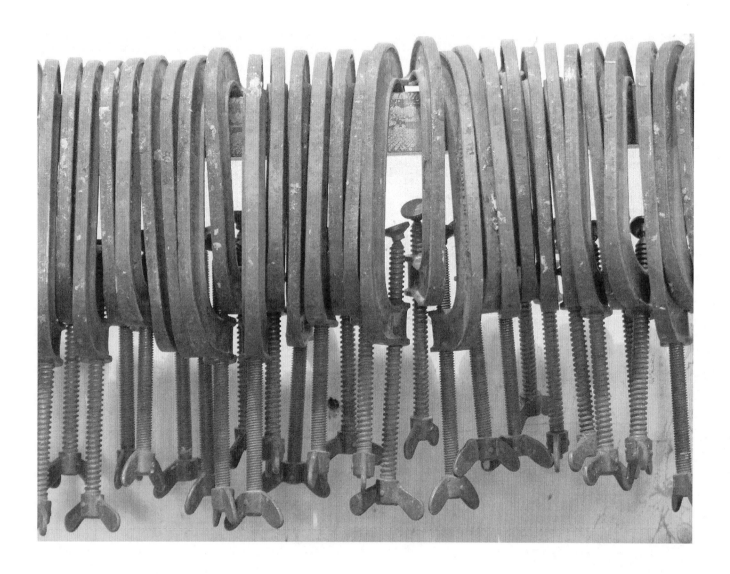

Fig 2.7 Clamps used for laminating

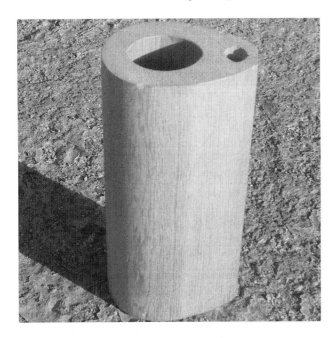

Fig 2.8 Sample yacht mast cross-section

Laminating Masts

Masts of up to 19 feet (5.79m) can be made from two lengths of spruce laminated together longitudinally; one side of the plank is flipped before being rejoined so that the internal stresses are balanced. Above this length, masts also require a Scarf joint to connect timber sections end to end. This joint is made by splicing the timber at an angle to increase the surface area of the cross-sections and by connecting the sections in such a way that they can resist tension, compression and torsion (twisting). Masts above 34 feet (10.36m) require complex laminations that can precisely control their flexibility under load.

The process of clamping and gluing the timber is carefully controlled and monitored, and a range of clamps and vices is used to apply the precise amount of pressure along the mast. Mast-makers

Fig 2.9 Sample yacht mast cross-section

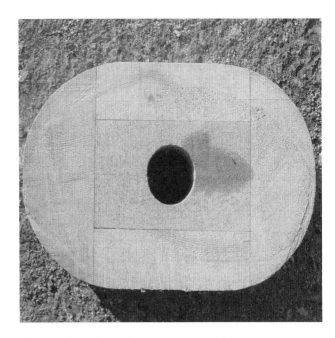

Fig 2.10 Sample yacht mast cross-section

Fig 2.11 Sample sections in Sitka spruce

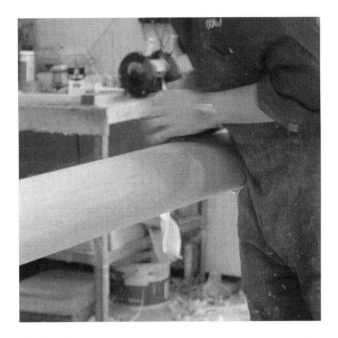

Fig 2.12 Hand planing

still use traditional glues such as Arolite 300, which is a two part glue consisting of a resin and hardener that are applied separately to each surface. It is sometimes desirable to have a glue line showing on the surface of the mast for aesthetic reasons.

Shaping
Much of the work of shaping masts and rowing oars is done by hand, from rough cutting the profile of the mast with a drawknife, to planing the surface finish. Planing tools are individually shaped according to the different profiles to be worked on.

These profiles can be many and varied. Oars can range in size from 6 feet (1.82m) to 17 feet (5.18m) and come in shapes such as double sided flat bladed, laminated spoon bladed (with round or 'D' section loom), fine bladed (with hollow or scalloped loom), pin type or paddle shaped.

Fig 2.13 Hand planing

Fig 2.14 Bespoke planing tools

Fig 2.15 Mast making

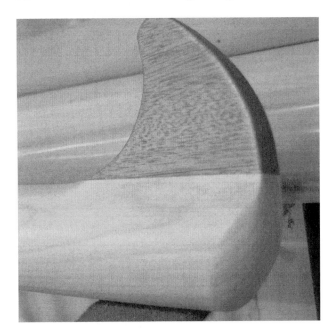

Fig 2.16 Paddle detail

To calculate the length of an oar in relation to the size of the vessel, take the beam of the boat, add 8 feet 5 inches (2.56m), divide by 2, and then multiply by 2.45.

The Fabricator
F.Collar first started making oars and masts in the 1930s and 1950s respectively. The company supplied the racing oars for every Olympic Games from 1952 to 1984, producing 200 identical masts for the Mexico Olympics in 1968. They have built masts up to 60 feet (18.2m) long, and have an archive of over 300 design drawings. The first job of every new apprentice is to make a set of bespoke planing tools.

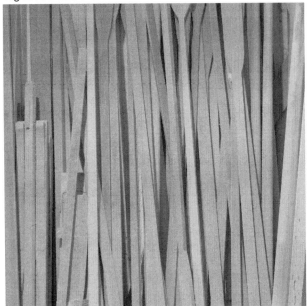

Fig 2.17 Oar 'blanks'

Fig 2.18 Paddles await varnishing

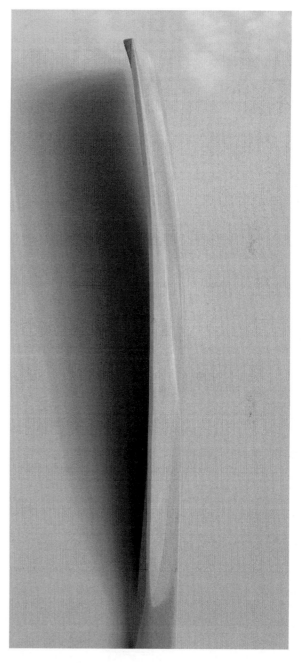

Fig 2.19 Finished racing oar

3

Glass-Reinforced Plastic

Fig 3.0 Preparing chopped strand mat

Fig 3.1 Strand mat, cut and labelled, ready for laminating

Glass-Reinforced Plastic
GRP Solutions, Poole

Fibreglass
As with any pouring or moulding process, the act of casting shapes out of fluid materials has the advantage that complex, curved surfaces may be achieved. Large-scale structural components are now commonly manufactured out of resins that are reinforced with fibreglass. The fibreglass is built up in layers inside the liquid resin - a process known here as laminating - and products are often further reinforced with layers of foam, Kevlar or carbon fibre for extra stiffening.

The fibreglass itself is a material woven from extremely fine fibres of glass. It is commonly used in the manufacture of insulation and textiles, and is also used as a reinforcing agent for many plastic

Fig 3.2 Fibreglass with chopped strand mat fibre - detail

Fig 3.3 Moulded GRP steering console

Fig 3.4 Sacrificial trim detail in mould

Fig 3.5 Resin - detail

products, the result being a composite material called Glass-Reinforced Plastic (GRP), also known as Glass-fibre Reinforced Epoxy (GRE). Fibreglass is usually supplied in the form of matting known as chopped strand mat, which is an unwoven fabric.

A resin is a plastic material that can change its state from liquid to solid under certain conditions, e.g. through adding a catalyst or hardener or due to a temperature change. GRP uses epoxy resins which are strong high performance waterproof resins that are resistant to environmental degradation. As opposed to resins which are cured by a catalyst, epoxy resins are a two part adhesive in which the resin is mixed together with a hardener.

The Plug
The final form of a GRP product relies upon the mould from which it is cast. The plug is the master

Fig 3.6 Plug has served its purpose

Fig 3.7 Storage liner, ready for release from mould

Fig 3.8 Foam cores, cut to shape

pattern from which the casting mould is created. Not only must the plug be accurate but it must be designed in such a way that the final cast can easily be removed from the mould. Often this will mean breaking it down into a series of smaller plugs that are designed so that their castings can then be assembled together to make the whole. (This may also be necessary for transportation purposes.)

The plug is usually made from timber, but a variety of materials can be incorporated depending on the geometry of the form. It is a critical part of the process that often requires ingenuity on the part of the fabricator - to turn the client's ideas into three-dimensional form and then to go on and make a 1:1 prototype. Rough frames are erected and then skinned, often with plywood, and the entire surface is then filled and faired by hand until the required form is achieved and any blemishes removed.

Fig 3.9 Foam cores, cut to shape

Fig 3.10 Surface finishing work

Fig 3.11 Cast GRP showing structural reinforcing details

Fig 3.12 Ship's fuel tank 1800mm x 3600mm/6' x 12'

Fig 3.13 Ship's fuel tank 1800mm x 3600mm/6' x 12'

The Mould

The mould is cast from the plug and becomes the (negative) die from which the final product is manufactured. Moulds are either open or closed type according to the type of product the cost involved and the frequency of use.

With the more traditional Open Moulds, the process of laminating the fibreglass matting is known as 'hand lay-up'. Waxes are applied to the surface of the mould as a releasing agent so that the GRP can easily be separated after it has set; the process of casting then starts with the application of a coat of resin known as the gelcoat. Gelcoats are barrier coatings that can produce finished surfaces with high gloss, colour and surface integrity retention after years of environmental exposure.

The gelcoat eventually becomes the outer surface

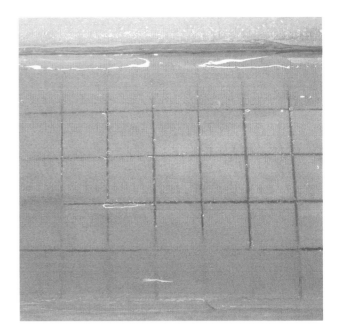

Fig 3.14 Foam cores in the form of cellular sheets

Fig 3.15 Fuel tank detail

Fig 3.16 Surface finishing work

Fig 3.17 Detail of polished GRP surface

of the object and is capable of displaying colour and fine detail down to the level of texturing. Once the gelcoat has begun hardening (to protect the mould from the glass) the process of laminating begins - this is known as 'wetting out'. Fibreglass matting that has been cut to shape is pressed firmly into place, and liquid resin is applied by brush or roller. The process is then repeated until the required number of laminations is achieved. At this stage, a layer of foam may be sandwiched with other layers of GRP to form a stiff, composite material. These foam cores can either be cut out from solid panels or are supplied in the form of cellular, flexible sheets.

Spray lay-up: Open moulds can also employ a 'spray lay-u" technique, where a spray gun is used for the simultaneous deposition of chopped glass and catalysed resin onto the surface of the mould.

Closed moulds: This technique is now becoming more common as control over the curing of the catalytic resin is more accurate in a closed mould.

The Fabricator
GRP Solutions was established by John Rawson in 1992. Known for their ability to engage with unusual and complex projects, their work combines repeat production runs of items such as storage boxes and ship's fuel tanks with one-off, bespoke castings of anything from a 5m diameter dome to the steering console for a modern powerboat.

Fig 3.18 Polished product

4

Tensile Steel

Fig 4.0 Steel wire is fed into the winding mechanisms

Tensile Steel
Ormiston Wire Company, Isleworth

Wire Rope
Wire rope is manufactured in many ways and in several grades according to its use. Relying chiefly on the grade - the quality - of the raw steel wire, a manufacturer can nevertheless vary the structure and composition of the rope and thus change its qualities of strength and flexibility. Wire rope has finite limitations in size, due to weight and handling.

Wires, Strands and Cores
Wire rope is normally made from cold drawn, carbon steel wires. Individual wires are helically twisted into strands which are in turn twisted around a central core to form the rope or cable. Cores are made from various natural and synthetic fibres such as hemp, cotton, Kevlar and aramide, PVC or wire.

Fig 4.1 Machine for winding individual wires into a strand

Fig 4.2 Steel wire is supplied on bobbins

Fig 4.3 Steel wires come together to form a single strand

Fig 4.4 Steel wires come together to form a single strand

Moving Parts

The strength and flexibility of the rope is controlled by the size of the individual wires, the number used to form a strand, and the number of strands used to form the rope. The standard combinations are known as 6 x 7, 6 x 19, 6 x 37 and 8 x 19 (extra flexible), where the first number denotes strands and the second denotes wires per strand - more complex ropes may in fact consist of literally hundreds of moving parts.

Direction

Wire rope can be made either 'right lay' or 'left lay' according to the direction in which the wires and strands are travelling. Where the strands and rope are each coiled in opposing directions, the rope is known as 'regular lay'. Where they are wound the same way, the rope is known as 'lang lay'. An 18 x 7 Non-rotating Rope, for example, is fabricated by

Fig 4.5 Winding machine - active

Fig 4.6 Wire rope

Fig 4.7 Winding machine - static

Fig 4.8 Wire fed from spools into the winding mechanisms

Fig 4.9 Feeding a Kevlar core into the winding machine

laying eighteen, seven wire strands around a hemp core in two concentric layers, the inside layer consisting of six strands laid in one direction and the outside layer consisting of 12 strands laid in the opposite direction.

Finishes

Rope made from bare steel wires with no coating is known as 'bright', and relies upon the protection of the lubricants used in its formation. For extra corrosion protection, the steel may be galvanised (where all of the wires are coated in pure zinc) or plastic (PVC) coated.

Production

All rope production is by automated machinery consisting of highly complex winding mechanisms. The demands on the fabricator are such that he/she will constantly be seeking to adapt and improve

Fig 4.10 Braided wire

Fig 4.11 Winding machine - active

Fig 4.12 Winding machines - Ormiston Wire Company

them to suit their purpose. This is part of the long-standing history of the reciprocal relationship between machine tool manufacturers and their operators, which entails contant refinement and adjustment for optimisation and ease of use.

Stockwire
Steel (spring, stainless, mild, galvanised), copper, brass, phosphor bronze, aluminium, lead, tin, nickel and tungsten.

Stock Braids*
Plain copper, tinned copper and aluminium.
*Braid construction: 24/10/0.2mm means 24 bobbins with 10 wires per bobbin, wire size 0.2mm

Fig 4.13 Winding machines - Ormiston Wire Company

Fig 4.14 Wire rope can vary in both strength and flexibility

Fig 4.15 Winding mechanism

Fig 4.16 Braided wire

The Fabricator

Ormiston Wire Company Ltd was founded in 1793 in the City of London and is now in its sixth generation. The company is currently based in Isleworth, West London where they manufacture specialised wires, braids, and strands in many different metals and in batches ranging from 1m to 44,000km. This family firm still maintains the motto 'any kind of wire', and produce wire ranging from surgical suture wire smaller than a human hair to polypropylene covered, Kevlar-cored strand, for low-voltage lighting. The company also supplies a wide range of wire rope fittings used for suspension systems, e.g. ferrules and clamps.

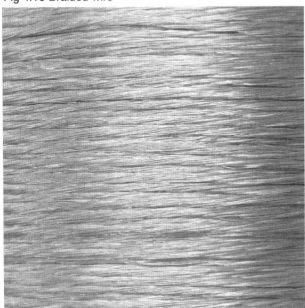

Fig 4.17 Wire rope

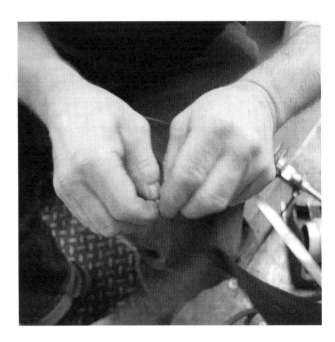

Fig 4.18 Finishing wire ends

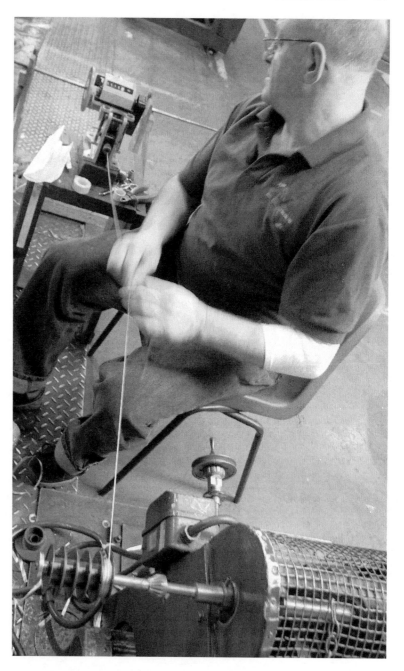

Fig 4.19 Measuring lengths of wire onto spools

5

Steel Sections

Fig 5.0 Steel stock

Steel Sections
Simon Veglio, Mitcham (Fabricating)
The Angle Ring Company, Tipton (Bending)

Steel Sections
Steel is a product of coal, iron ore and limestone, and is manufactured in a number of stages. The coal is rid of its impurities - transformed into coke - and mixed with iron ore and limestone in a blast furnace in which it is heated to several thousand degrees to produce liquid iron (the limestone carries impurities to the surface and is skimmed off to become slag). The iron produced in a blast furnace is known as pig iron and is strong but very brittle. To convert iron into steel (which is strong but flexible) the proportion of carbon in the mix must be adjusted by blowing hot air or pure oxygen into molten iron. The liquid steel is then cast into either a slab shape or into a linear shape known as a billet or bloom.

Fig 5.1 Section of a large fabricated beam

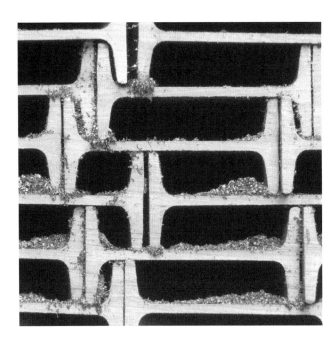

Fig 5.2 Universal beams ready for fabricating

Fig 5.3 Universal beam with chalked-on dimensions

Fig 5.4 Fly-press for hand bending and forming of steel

These shapes are then reheated so that the slabs can be rolled into flat steel plates and the billets can be squeezed into linear sections. In addition to this hot rolling process, most steel products then undergo further processing in the cold state. Cold rolling steel involves passing a strip of steel through a series of pressurised rolling mills and has the effect of reducing its thickness to a higher tolerance while significantly improving its performance characteristics. Steel used for construction purposes is standard carbon steel, having up to 0.3% carbon and known as mild steel.

Universal Sections
There is a standard range of available 'hot-rolled steel sections' or universal sections. These include beams, joists, columns, angles, channels, Tees and hollow sections with circular, square, rectangular, and elliptical cross-sections (see Fig 5.10.)

Fig 5.5 Pillar drill

Fig 5.6 Drill bits

Fig 5.7 Mechanical hacksaw for the accurate cutting of small steel sections

Fig 5.8 Arc welding of steel plate onto a UB

Fig 5.9 Welding equipment

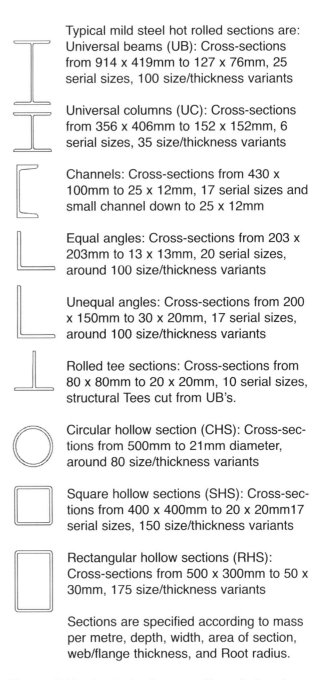

Typical mild steel hot rolled sections are:
Universal beams (UB): Cross-sections from 914 x 419mm to 127 x 76mm, 25 serial sizes, 100 size/thickness variants

Universal columns (UC): Cross-sections from 356 x 406mm to 152 x 152mm, 6 serial sizes, 35 size/thickness variants

Channels: Cross-sections from 430 x 100mm to 25 x 12mm, 17 serial sizes and small channel down to 25 x 12mm

Equal angles: Cross-sections from 203 x 203mm to 13 x 13mm, 20 serial sizes, around 100 size/thickness variants

Unequal angles: Cross-sections from 200 x 150mm to 30 x 20mm, 17 serial sizes, around 100 size/thickness variants

Rolled tee sections: Cross-sections from 80 x 80mm to 20 x 20mm, 10 serial sizes, structural Tees cut from UB's.

Circular hollow section (CHS): Cross-sections from 500mm to 21mm diameter, around 80 size/thickness variants

Square hollow sections (SHS): Cross-sections from 400 x 400mm to 20 x 20mm17 serial sizes, 150 size/thickness variants

Rectangular hollow sections (RHS): Cross-sections from 500 x 300mm to 50 x 30mm, 175 size/thickness variants

Sections are specified according to mass per metre, depth, width, area of section, web/flange thickness, and Root radius.

Fig 5.10 Table showing basic range of hot-rolled sections

Fig 5.11 Cropping machine for cutting and punching small sections

Fig 5.12 Angle grinder for removing and smoothing welds

Steel Fabrication

Steel sections can be cut to length with mechanical hacksaws, and some types (e.g. bars) can be folded using manual press brakes. Steel is assembled using a variety of processes according to the design and use of the product. It can be connected together by drilling and bolting (a process that can permit tolerance for adjustment or disassembly) or, for a permanent fusion, by brazing, gluing, or welding. Welding is the only way of joining two or more pieces of metal to make them act as a single piece.

A weld joins metals by applying heat, sometimes with pressure and sometimes with an intermediate, molten, filler metal. By applying intense heat, metal at the joint between two parts is melted and caused to intermix. Once cool, welds can be ground flat using an abrasive wheel known as an angle grinder.

Fig 5.13 Magnetic drill providing accurate site drilling

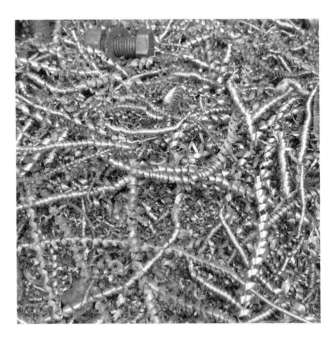

Fig 5.14 Metal burr

Fig 5.15 Oxygen and butane gas cutting gear

Fig 5.16 Welded steel angle frame (weld to be ground)

The most common methods of fusing metals in this way are ARC and MIG welding.

ARC Welding
An electronic arc creates the intense heat required to melt the metal. The arc is formed between the metal and an electrode (rod or wire) that is manually or mechanically guided along the joint. Often, the rod or wire not only conducts the current but also melts and supplies filler metal to the joints.

MIG Welding
A MIG (Metal Inert Gas) weld is made when an aluminium alloy wire is used as a combined electrode and filler material. This is a semi-automatic process that feeds a continuous spool of filler wire to the weld bead by magnetic forces as small droplets - a process known as spray transfer - and enables welding from any position.

Fig 5.17 Steel brackets formed on the fly-press

Fig 5.18 Basic tools like a vice are vital in the workshop

Fig 5.19 Fabricated steel balcony rail, primed and ready for painting

Fig 5.20 Stock universal steel sections

Bending Steel Sections

It was the advent of universal sections in 1958 that led to the development of tooling able to bend the full range of structural steel, i.e. angles, flats, bars, tees, split tees, beams, columns, joists, castellated beams, tubes, pipes and all other available hollow sections including elliptical and semi-elliptical tubes.

Cold Rolling

The cold rolling process involves passing a steel section through a specially adapted set of three rollers. With each pass of the rollers a measurable pressure is applied by the third adjustable roller, producing an even radius along the rolled length. This process is repeated until the correct curvature is achieved. For smaller sections the pressure is applied by hand through a leverage mechanism. For larger sections the machines are pre-programmed to a defined pressure that relates to the sectional

Fig 5.21 Stock hollow sections, bar and angle

Fig 5.22 Rolled channel sections

Fig 5.23 Cold rolling a Universal Beam (UB) section

Fig 5.24 Detail showing a RHS being cold rolled

dimensions, weight and the desired radius. This process is not to be confused with cold rolled steel products, which are fabricated with rollers from thin sheets of flat steel and include metal stud members and lightweight columns and beams.

Three-Dimensional Bending
With multiple passes of the cold rolling process in different sectional planes, the fabricator is able to produce curves or bends in more than one dimension. This helical rolling process can bend a spiral in structural steel.

Beams of up to 1100mm deep and tubes of up to 915mm diameter can be bent to shape. The longest single piece of steel, that can be rolled is 28m long and is manufactured by Corus (formerly British Steel). A tolerance of 3mm can be achieved along the length of such a beam.

Fig 5.25 Detail of small section rolling machine

Fig 5.26 Detail of small section rolling machine

Fig 5.27 Some three dimensionally rolled channel sections

Fig 5.28 Rolled CHS tubes

Hot Bending

Hot induction bending can produce smaller radii, and there is less local deformation of the steel. For example a 533mm x 210mm 101kg/m beam can be curved to a radii of less than 4m with hot bending as opposed to a 25m limit with cold rolling.

Hot Induction-Bending

In the hot induction bending process the steel section is passed through an electric coil. The coil produces a strong magnetic field inducing electrical currents in the steel, which locally heat up the steel in a 'red hot' band across the material. The leading end of the steel section is clamped to a pivoted radius arm, which can be adjusted in length for the desired radii. The steel is pushed through the induction coil by giant hydraulic rams.

Fig 5.29 Detail of hot Induction-bending machine

Fig 5.30 Detail of induction coil

Fig 5.31 Hot induction-bending machine forming a large CHS steel tube

Fig 5.32 Plate roller

Plate Rolling and Forming

Plate rolling is another cold rolling process for forming sheets of plate steel. The plates are horizontally fed through a large three roller 'mangle', which through controllable pressure deforms the sheet with each pass of the machine.

Plate steel of up to 200mm thick can be rolled up to a width of 750mm.

Plates of 35mm thick can be rolled up to widths of 3050mm.

Press Braking

Press brakes are employed for pressing and folding plate steel for custom structural sections, tubes and plates. Larger presses can deliver 1200 tonnes of pressure and can shape steel plate of up to 200mm deep and up to 10m in length.

Fig 5.33 Press brake with a capacity of 1200 tonnes

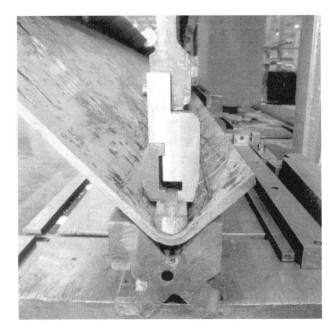

Fig 5.34 Detail of press brake

Fig 5.35 Rolled large section tubes with welds clearly visible

Fig 5.36 Rolling small steel rod hoops by hand

The Fabricators

Simon Veglio has been a steel fabricator for more than 20 years, working closely with architects and artists on a range of projects from sculpture, steel staircases and railings to bespoke structural steelwork for new-build and refurbishment schemes.

The Angle Ring company began as their name suggests by rolling small steel angles sections into rings for chimney stiffeners and motor casing supports. Established in 1951 Angle Ring is one of only a few specialised firms worldwide dedicated to the 'post-forming' or bending of plate steel and hot rolled steel sections.

Fig 5.37 Angle rings, the original product still in production

Fig 5.38 Angle Ring Ltd

Fig 5.39 Some demonstration test pieces for exhibitions and trade shows

6

Limestone

Fig 6.0 Durlston Formation, Isle of Purbeck, Dorset

Fig 6.1 Quarried stone, piled up to dry out

Limestone
D & P Quarries Ltd, Swanage (Fabricating)

Pubeck Limestone
There are over 200 beds of Purbeck stone in what is known as the Durlston Formation on the Isle of Purbeck in Dorset. This Cretaceous rock has been quarried since mediaeval times, originally in underground quarries accessed from shafts and now excavated by the open cast method. Stone is cleaved from the beds using mechanical excavators and piled up on the surface to dry out.

'Working' Stone
The oldest building material known to man is still one of the few that is transformed into a product at source. Different beds produce different sizes and quality of stone, and this will determine the way in which the stone is acted upon. Stone may be sawn,

Fig 6.2 Surface of unworked stone

Fig 6.3 Stone being transported from open cast quarry

Fig 6.4 Unworked stone blocks

cropped, split or chiselled into shape, resulting in a range of building products with different functions, forms and finishes.

Cropping Stone

Smaller beds produce stone that is commonly used for (dry or wet laid) walling. The quarried stone is cropped to size using a guillotine and can then either be sold directly for use as boundary walling or hammer dressed (roughly squared) for use on the outer face of cavity walls.

Fig 6.5 Stone prepared for use as building blocks

Fig 6.6 Larger blocks will be cut into slabs

Fig 6.7 Guillotining quarried stone blocks

Fig 6.8 Hacksaw blades

Sawn Stone
Large-scale, high quality blocks are sawn into shape using a range of mechanical saws. A multi-bladed frame saw will carve a block of stone into a set of slabs in roughly 6 hours, while diamond-bladed circular saws enable precision cutting: the saw blades follow a laser line, can operate in various axes, and are also used to mill or route precise geometric incisions from the surface of the stone. These tools can also work to a CAD generated program.

Fig 6.9 Multi-bladed mechanical hacksaw

Fig 6.10 Stone slabs, cut by mechanical saw

Fig 6.11 600mm diamond-bladed circular saw

Fig 6.12 Mobile bench for use with circular saw

Finishing

The fossil structure of each stone is different. Some stones are made up of thousands of densely packed tiny shells, some have larger shells more widely spaced out, while others contain no fossils at all. Probably the most famous bed of Purbeck stone is known as Purbeck marble. Though not a true marble, it has a variety of colours and, as with most Purbeck stone, is hard and dense and can therefore be polished to produce a very durable surface finish. Grinding and polishing machines have interchangeable tools with different abrasive capacities. The stone may also be hand finished using chisels, or even turned.

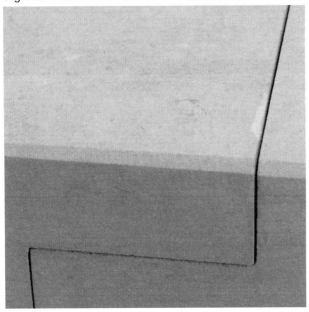

Fig 6.13 Fine detail in interlocking stone blocks

Fig 6.14 Finished stone blocks

Fig 6.15 CNC circular saw

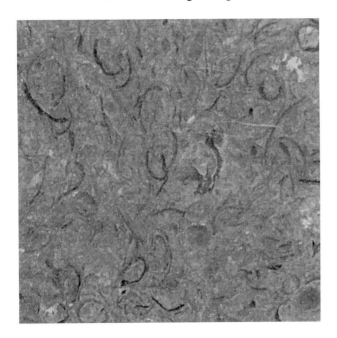

Fig 6.16 Surface finish on polished stone

The Fabricator

D. & P. Lovell Quarries Ltd produce a variety of building stones as well as a range of architectural features including quoins, jambs, lintels, arches, mullions, corbels and copings. Downs Quarry is one of the few privately owned quarries in Purbeck, and the company produce their own range of hand-carved, ornamental stone as well as one-off building products to order. They stock a range of imported stone, and supply directly from quarry to site.

Fig 6.17 Surface finish on polished stone

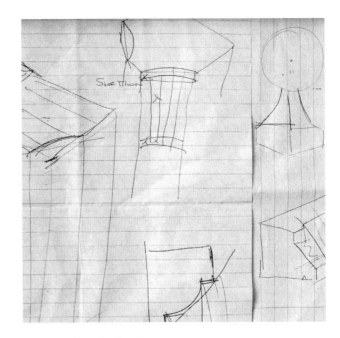

Fig 6.18 Sketch of cutting sequence

Fig 6.19 Automated stone polishing

7

Terrazzo Concrete

Fig 7.0 Crushed stone aggregate

Fig 7.1 Crushed stone aggregate - detail

Terrazzo Concrete
Pallam Pre-Cast, Enfield

Terrazzo
Terrazzo concrete has been around for several hundred years. From the Italian word for terrace, terrazzo originated as a new use for discarded remnants of marble. They were embedded into clay terraces and subsequently ground flat. Terrazzo floors are extremely hardwearing and can last for hundreds of years.

With the development of concrete and grinding tools many more types of material can be embedded, from fibre-optic cables to stainless steel and brass strips, and many forms and finishes can be achieved. As with concrete, terrazzo can be fabricated in-situ or in pre-cast units, with its use limited only by the skill of the mould maker.

Fig 7.2 White Portland cement permits the addition of dye

Fig 7.3 Mixing and measuring dyes/pigments

Fig 7.4 Mixing cement, water and aggregates into a slurry

Concrete

Concrete is made from Portland cement combined with an aggregate and mixed together with water to create a mouldable slurry. Aggregate consists of naturally occurring materials such as crushed or uncrushed gravel, sand and stone chippings, and these may be combined in various proportions. Marble aggregates come in eight graded sizes ranging from 3mm to 25m.

Terrazzo can be precast and factory finished or cast in-situ and polished on site. Terrazzo has a base or core layer and a facing layer of not less than 10mm. The base layer usually consists of a mix of three parts aggregate to one part cement, with the facing layer having a 2:1 mix. The facing aggregate is also likely to include more of a finer element such as sand, as well as using white cement which enables mineral colour pigments to be added to the mix.

Fig 7.5 Cement 'batch' mixer

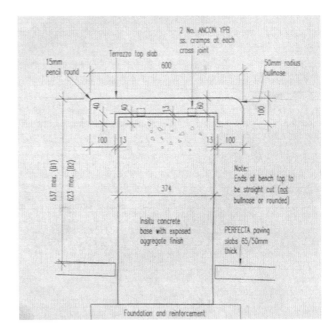

Fig 7.6 Section drawing used for designing formwork

Fig 7.7 Timber formwork is set out on benches

Fig 7.8 Rolled edges are formed using cement fillets

According to its use, the core layer may also be reinforced with mild or stainless steel bars to provide the concrete with the tensile strength necessary for structural loading.

Formwork
Formwork is the name given to the mould from which the terrazzo concrete is cast. The setting out and construction of the formwork is a highly skilled job. Formwork is made predominantly from timber, and it is therefore a carpenter who translates the design drawings into a three-dimensional mould. Details such as curved edges can be achieved through applying quick-drying cement to the edges of the mould in the form of a fillet.

Releasing agents are applied to the surface of the formwork before the slurry is poured. The concrete must then be vibrated either manually or by

Fig 7.9 Reinforcing bars have been cast in

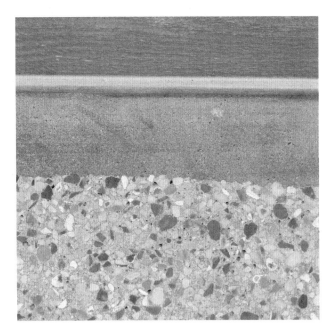

Fig 7.10 Terrazzo concrete - edge detail

Fig 7.11 Casting the terrazzo mix, hand trowelled into mould/formwork

Fig 7.12 Grinding tools have different abrasive strength

mechanical means in order to remove air bubbles by bringing them to the surface. Terrazzo can be removed from the formwork after 48 hours but must be cured for a further 24 hours before grinding.

Grinding and Polishing
There is little shrinkage during the drying-out process; however, formwork must be constructed with sufficient tolerance to allow for grinding and polishing of the facing layers - the larger the aggregate, the greater the depth of surface that will be lost through grinding. As much as 15mm may be lost. Even after vibrating concrete there are still small air pockets and these will become visible on the surface after grinding. Surfaces must therefore be grouted with a matching mix before the final stage of grinding and polishing. Grinding of terrazzo is usually carried out by the wet method, where abrasive blocks are rotated against the terrazzo

Fig 7.13 Fully automated grinding machine

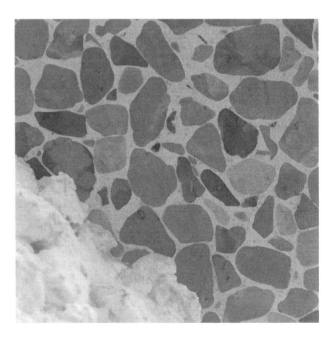

Fig 7.14 Terrazzo concrete - surface detail

Fig 7.15 Polishing the surface with grinding wheels

Fig 7.16 Terrazzo concrete - corner/edge detail

surface with a constant stream of water from the machine head. Surface finishes can be rough, textured, smooth or polished - a range of blocks give different levels of abrasion. Final polishing is carried out using water and fine grit stones.

The Fabricator

Pallam Pre-Cast is a sister company to the QM Natural Stone and Design Company. The company was started in 1979 by Carlo Fossaluzza (himself from a long line of stone craftsmen), and now offers a wide range of expertise on the materials and processes associated with terrazzo, marble and mosaic. The company advise upon design and working with artists, and designers are able to manufacture bespoke products to order, stocking a huge range of samples including natural stone, glass, metal aggregates and mineral dyes.

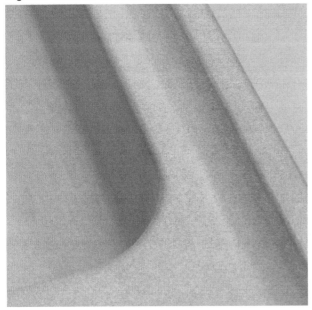

Fig 7.17 Terrazzo concrete - geometric detail

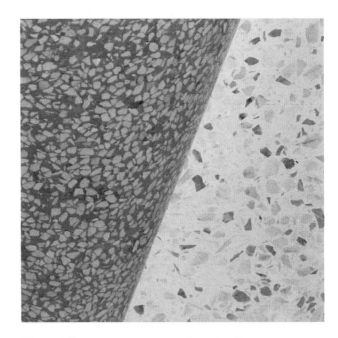

Fig 7.18 Terrazzo concrete - surface detail

Fig 7.19 Pre-cast concrete bench

8

Membrane Fabric

Fig 8.0 Fabric is supplied in rolls of up to 2400mm

Fig 8.1 PVC-coated polyester

Membrane Fabric
Lindstrand Technologies, Oswestry

Fabric Engineering
Until recently architectural fabric engineering has been mainly confined to either single skin structures that are tensioned between compressive structures e.g. the Millennium Dome, or superpressure structures which maintain their shape by pumping air into the structure, e.g. tennis halls.

Air Cells
An air cell structure is one that is self-supportable and self-erectable using only an air fan - it is constructed entirely from fabric and can therefore be reduced to a small volume for handling and transportation. The fabric is held in place under tension from the internal, compressive force of air under pressure, while the cellular nature of the structure

Fig 8.2 Drop stitch fabric, a double skinned fabric

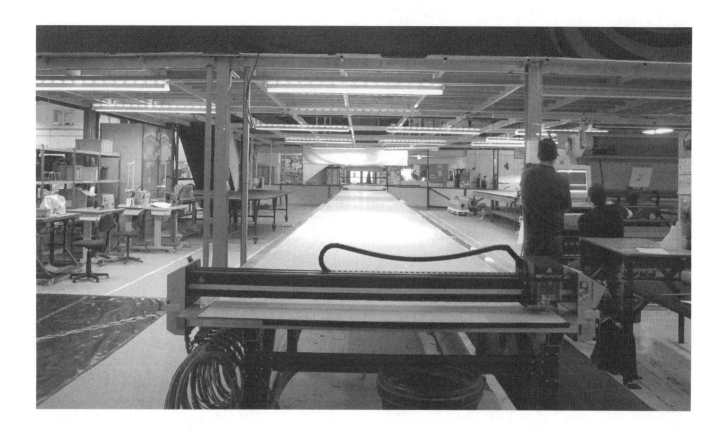

Fig 8.3 Cutting bench for automated pattern cutter

Fig 8.4 Cutting tool head with a hole punch and wheel

offers an enormous range of geometrical variations including the capacity to be self-supporting and to resist wind load.

Membrane Fabrics

'Polymerisation' is the last in a series of chemical processes needed to create the molecular chains that form polyvinyl chloride (PVC). PVC is a thermoplastic and is produced in the form of a white powder that is blended with other ingredients to form a range of synthetic products. Additives consist of heat stabilisers and lubricants as well as those that will determine mechanical properties such as flexibility.

Membrane fabrics are made from PVC-coated polyester. These synthetic fabrics are strong in tension and resistant to shear, and there is a range of around 20 standard colours. They are light,

Fig 8.5 Automated pattern cutting

Fig 8.6 Polyester strips

Fig 8.7 Fabric is vacuum held onto cutting bench

Fig 8.8 Workstation for stitching and sewing

flameproof and have a maximum thickness of about 1.2mm. UV light and weathering will cause deterioration in the fabrics over a period of 10 to 20 years according to climate.

Pattern Cutting

The process of fabricating air cell structures is akin to that of tailoring. The polyester fabric is delivered in anything up to 2.4m wide rolls, and panels can be cut by automated cutting machines according to CAD profiles. These CNC cutters have a variety of interchangeable heads (consisting of a hole punch and cutting wheel) while the 21m benches along which they travel are designed to vacuum the fabric onto the cutting surface for precision cutting.

Stitching and Welding

Once panels have been cut to size they are assembled in a series of operations. Panels are

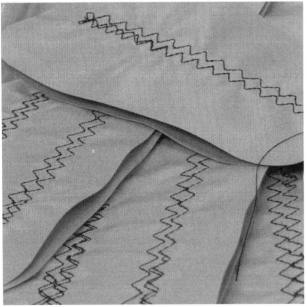

Fig 8.9 Structural stitching together of fabric pieces

Fig 8.10 Tethering detail

Fig 8.11 Lindstrand Technologies Limited

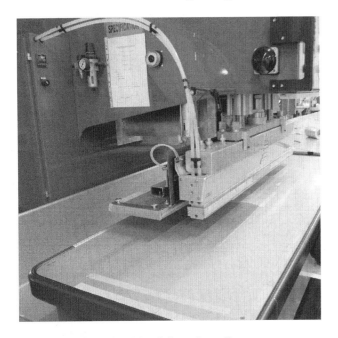

Fig 8.12 Welding machine follows laser line

drop-stitched together to create a structural, three-dimensional framework, while the overall envelope is seam-welded. Welding techniques depend upon the precise nature of the fabric and the overall geometry. One of the characteristics of thermoplastics is that sheets or panels can be fused together through melting and cooling. This can be acheived through the use of hot air delivered by a machine that simultaneously compresses the two sheets using a rolling action. Alternatively high-frequency welding joins surfaces by heating on contact with the electrodes of a high frequency electrical generator.

Details

Air cell structures require points of stiffening and re-enforcing, either for intrinsic structural reasons or for connections, e.g. tethering and anchorage. They also require connections for air intake and

Fig 8.13 Applying adhesive for reinforcing details

Fig 8.14 Mobile heat-welding units

Fig 8.15 Inflated air cell

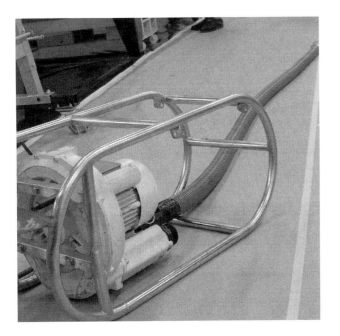

Fig 8.16 Air fans can react to a pressure drop

extraction. The fans used in air cell buildings normally operate on full power during inflation, but will then switch to intermittent mode and react only in response to a pressure drop.

Pneumatic Structures

Air inflated structures consist of pressurised cells forming structural tubes (air beams) to support a structure. Air inflated structures can work under high and low pressures. A low pressure inflatable has a typical working pressure of $80kN/m^2$ - 12 pounds per square inch (psi) whereas a high pressure inflatable can have a working pressure of up to $700kN/m^2$ - 100 psi. Fig 8.19 shows a structure being inflated in the factory to test for airtightness.

Fig 8.17 Connection detail for air intake

Fig 8.18 Flexible, plastic air supply line

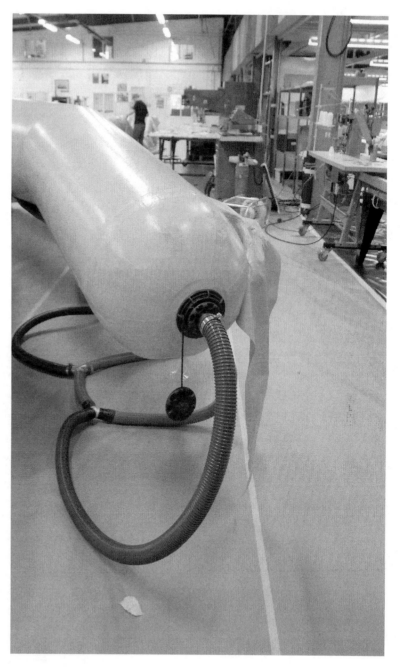

Fig 8.19 Air cell - factory testing

Fig 8.20 Air cell structure - entrance detail

The Fabricator
In December 1999 Lindstrand Technologies designed, built and erected the world's largest self-supporting fabric building for the Stockholm Millennium Project. Lindstrand is now prototyping a range of fabric structures from cold storage units for perishable food items to inflatable aircraft hangars, deployable 'clamshell' covers, airships and cargolifters. The company are also developing rapid-deployment systems such as tunnel plugs and flood-defence mechanisms.

Fig 8.21 Inflated air cell structure

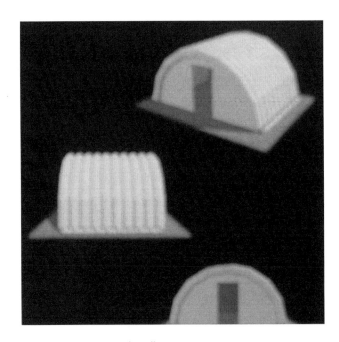

Fig 8.22 Prototype air cell structure

Fig 8.23 Factory testing

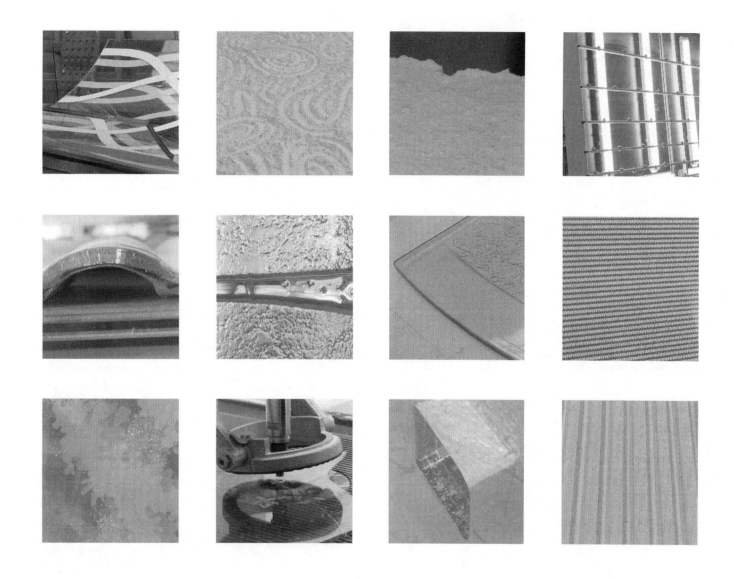

9

Float Glass

Fig 9.0 Standard, clear float glass

Float Glass
Fusion Glass Designs Ltd, London

Standard clear float glass is manufactured in a variety of sheet sizes and thicknesses, and can then be acted upon in a number of ways, which is known as secondary processing. Structurally, float glass can be tempered, annealed or laminated. Geometrically, it can be cut or formed into two-or three-dimensional curved surfaces. Decoratively, float glass can be textured, printed, etched or laminated with other sheet materials. Mechanically, it can be cut to shape, drilled for structural fixings, countersunk, or polished along its edges. Standard float glass is also available with a variety of body tints (blue, green, bronze and grey), can be low iron (ultra clear) or silvered, and can incorporate heat-gain and ultra-violet inhibitors in the form of adhesive films or sprays.

Fig 9.1 Suction device attached to overhead gantry

Fig 9.2 Machine for washing and drying glass sheets

Fig 9.3 Float glass awaits secondary processing

Fig 9.4 Machine for grinding smooth edges of sheet glass

Strengthening Glass:
Annealing
By controlling the rate at which molten glass cools, the stresses and strains that normally occur due to uneven shrinkage during cooling can be removed from the glass.

Tempering/Toughening
Glass is reheated and then the surfaces are rapidly cooled with jets of air. The inside core of the glass continues to cool and contract, forcing the surfaces into compression and the core into tension. When the glass breaks, the core releases tensile energy resulting in the formation of small glass granules.

Laminating
Layers of glass are bonded together with a resin interlayer to form a composite panel. If an outer layer breaks it is held in place by the substrate.

Fig 9.5 Glass is processed through the edging machine

Fig 9.6 Water-jet cutting of holes in glass

Fig 9.7 Automated pattern cutter - the tool heads are tiny grinding wheels

Fig 9.8 Kiln-fired texturing and screen printing

Cutting and Grinding

Glass can be cut to almost any geometric shape. Straight line cutting can be carried out by automated cutting machines that use grinding wheels. These machines operate in two axes and can be programmed to cut glass panels up to 6m long; benches use suction to hold the glass in place. Curved panels are cut by hand, using templates.

Straight edges are ground to an even finish by running the glass panels through grinding machines. Curves and more delicate details are hand polished with abrasive pads.

Shaping Glass

A flat sheet of glass when heated in the controlled environment of a kiln will liquefy - start to flow - at around 560°C. The glass will 'slump', through the

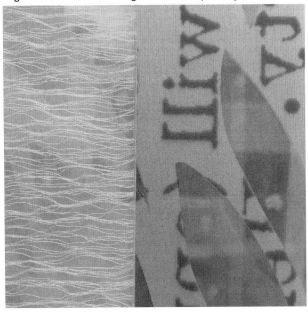

Fig 9.9 Printed and laminated glass with fabric interlayer

Fig 9.10 Printed and curved glass to a fixed radius

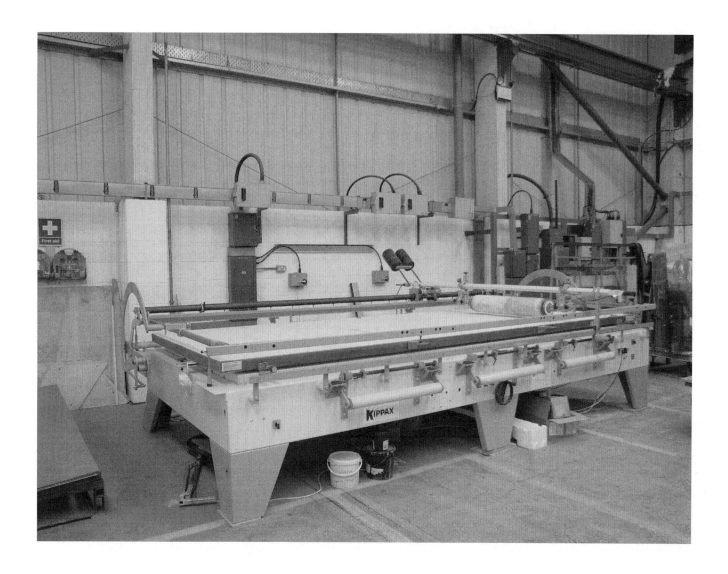

Fig 9.11 Screenprinting 'bed' for sheet glass

Fig 9.12 Casting plaster used for texture moulds

force of gravity, and hence can be moulded over a plaster form.At a large scale, entire panels can be curved in this way. The moulds, known as formworks, are constructed from sheet steel which has been rolled into shape and then mounted onto a timber framework. The glass panel is placed on top and the panel and formwork are placed in the kiln for firing.

At a small scale, glass panels can be textured or embossed by heating panels up to 760 degrees at which point the molten glass will flow into textured surfaces. Moulds are made using a combination of sieved, casting plaster (dry) and ceramic fibreboard. Stencils are delicately cut and carved by hand, while textures can be formed either by imprinting regular shapes into the casting plaster or by manipulating the plaster by hand, or by dusting. Areas left untextured are known as areas of 'resist'.

Fig 9.13 Effect of glass sheet on plaster mould

Fig 9.14 Regular profile mould

Fig 9.15 Mobile kiln

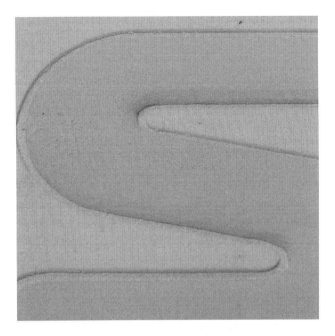

Fig 9.16 3D, hand-carved relief mould

Control of the kiln firing of textured glass is critical in terms of controlling shrinkage and ensuring that the glass flows exactly as desired. It can take as long as four days to achieve the desired effect. All kiln processes are subject to a maximum panel size of 3150mm x 1750mm, with thickness ranging from 6 to 25mm.

Decorating Glass
Float glass is delivered for secondary processing often having never been touched by hand. It is therefore machine washed and dried at various stages in the process.

Coating
Colours can be baked onto the surface of glass in a kiln. Colours can be applied as transparent, translucent (frosted) or opaque. Glass panels can also be screen printed or acid etched.

Fig 9.17 Textured board used as a mould

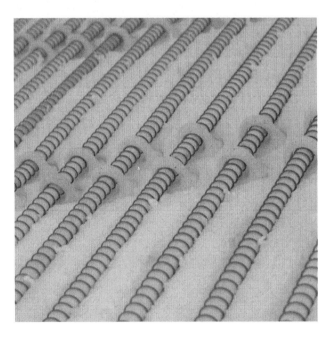

Fig 9.18 Heating elements, underside of kiln

Fig 9.19 Kiln is lowered into position

Fig 9.20 Kiln fired, profiled glass

Sandblasting

The effects of etching into the surface of glass range from simple frosting to finely stencilled patterns and deep carved 3-dimensional forms. The effect of sandblasting is to create an opaque or semi-opaque, non-reflecting surface which, being porous, is then treated with a polymer coating to form a protective barrier. Stencils range from computer and hand cut vinyl masks to screenprints and photographs. Sandblasting can be applied to any type of glass panel up to 5m x 3m.

Laminating

As well as the structural and safety advantages of laminating glass, the process of bonding layers of glass together can also incorporate a variety of interlayers such as opaque and transparent colours, fabrics, papers, veneers and meshes. Sheets of up to 3500mm x 1700mm can be laminated together.

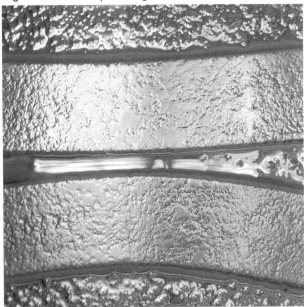

Fig 9.21 Kiln fired, textured glass

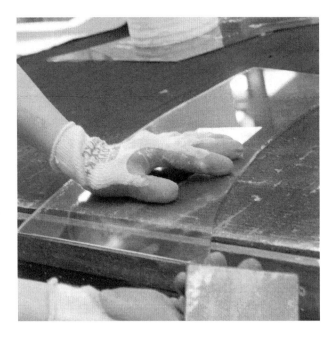

Fig 9.22 Complex shapes are hand ground and polished

Fig 9.23 Glass has been kiln textured using a plaster mould

Fig 9.24 Laminated glass with woven fabric interlayer

The Fabricator

Fusion Glass Designs Ltd have developed the facility to create innovative glass design by offering all of the processes described above in any combination. With so many variables, the company can offer bespoke products as well as a standard range of 25 textured finishes, eight fabric laminates, seven veneer laminates, 18 varieties of coloured kiln cast glass, and 29 coloured laminates. Their products, both bespoke and standard, are to be found in a wide range of architectural and interior design applications.

Fig 9.25 Edge detail in laminated glass

Fig 9.26 Geometric detail in laminated glass

Fig 9.27 Fusion Glass Limited

10

Tensile Yarns

Fig 10.0 Waste fibre

Tensile Yarns
Culzean Textile Solutions

Knitting and weaving are processes largely associated with clothing apparel, furnishing and bedding fabrics. Fabrics are, however, used for the substrate of GRP (Glass Reinforced Plastic) products including boats, tennis rackets, car parts and building components. The field of technical textiles or industrial Textiles describes the prototyping and fabrication of new textile solutions for industrial sectors as diverse as healthcare and the aerospace industry. Some of the areas of specialisation and development include fabric geometry, new combinations of fibre and yarn type, fibre densities and custom weaving and knitting techniques.

Fig 10.1 Yarn and fibre rack

Fig 10.2 Hanks of yarn mounted on a creel

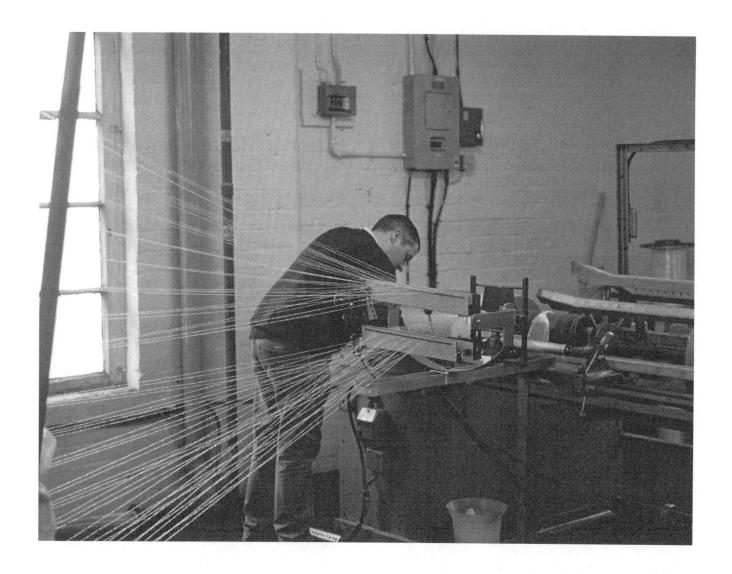

Fig 10.3 Sectional warping. The sections of warp are transferred to a beam to be fitted behind the loom

Fig 10.4 Horizontal warping mill

Materials
Many types of fibre and yarn are used in the fabricating processes of weaving, knitting and braiding. These fibres and yarns include:

Cottons, polymers, ceramics, glass-fibres, carbon fibres and metal wire. They also use trade named products such as Dyneema™ (a polyethylene fibre with a tensile strength 15 times that of steel), Kevlar™ and Nomex™.

Fibre: A type of material in an elongated form. A fibre type might be polyester, for instance.

Yarn: A prepared material that is categorised by weight, colour and properties such as the amount of twist, and whether the yarn has been texturised. Yarn is measured as grams per 1000m length, known as Tex or Tex count.

Fig 10.5 Tools for setting up the loom

Fig 10.6 Detail of machine braiding

Fig 10.7 Braiding machine with rotating bobbins forming a tubular braid

Fig 10.8 Loom with hanks of yarn

Weaving

A woven fabric consists of two sets of interlacing yarns at right angles. The warp yarns run the length of the fabric and the weft yarns, across the fabric. Woven fabrics are made on a loom, which hold the prepared warp yarns (see Fig10.10) in such a way as to allow the weft yarns to be passed across and in and out of the warp yarns to create a weave. Shuttle and twin-needle type looms are employed.

Knitting

Knitted fabrics are made from interlocking loops of yarn. The two basic knit types are weft knitting, by which process most knitted apparel is made, and warp knitting, a more complex process used to create denser, less pliable fabrics (see Fig 10.15) used as fibre reinforcement for composite structures. Single and double needlebed warp knitting and weft knitting facilities are employed.

Fig 10.9 Sections of warp being fed into loom

Fig 10.10 Cloth emerging from the loom

Fig 10.11 Detail of warp

Fig 10.12 Detail of woven heating tape

Braiding

Braids are fabric structures where each yarn interlaces with every other yarn, without any yarn making a complete twist around another. Braiding is used to make tubular fabrics and flat tapes such as heating tape (see Fig 10.2) and other custom, composite, reinforcement strips. Braids can comprise between 4 and 64 heads of yarn. (See Fig10.7 which shows a braiding machine.)

Fig 10.13 Detail of braiding machine 1

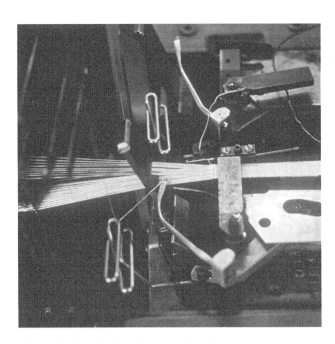

Fig 10.14 Detail of braiding machine 2

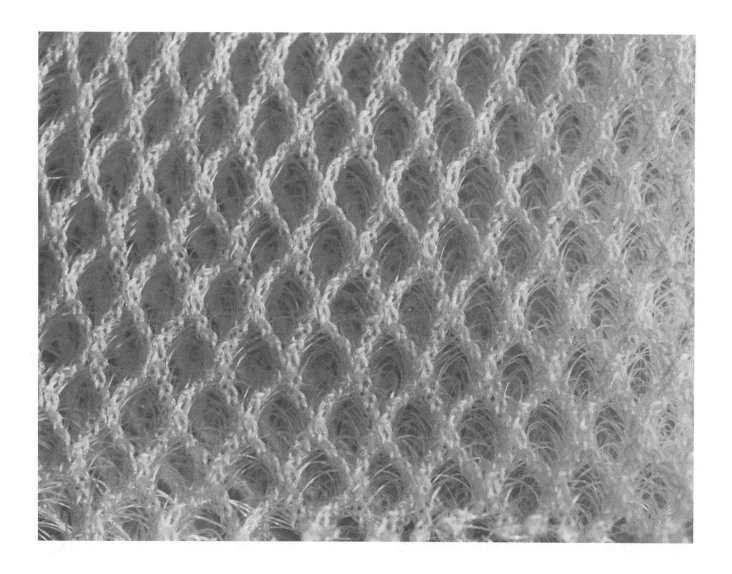

Fig 10.15 Detail of a knitted spacer fabric which can be used as a composite reinforcement substrate

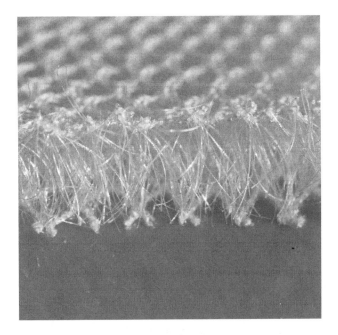

Fig 10.16 Edge of knitted spacer fabric

The Fabricator

We knit and weave everything except clothing.

Culzean Textile Solutions was established in 1985 by Michael Litton as a textile consulting service. Culzean has now expanded into a highly specialised technical textiles firm with prototyping and fabrication facilities. Culzean have developed products such as a space tether - a cosmic dust-resistant tether for satellite recovery, a artificial aorta - a knitted, bifurcated artery for human implant and the world's first one-piece, woven airbag without peripheral sewing. They have also developed 'spacer' fabrics, which are three-dimensional knitted fabrics consisting of two simultaneously produced surfaces with spring-like yarns connecting each side.

Fig 10.17 Knitted fabric made of steel wire

Fig 10.18 Fabric reinforced composite taxi 'coach spring'

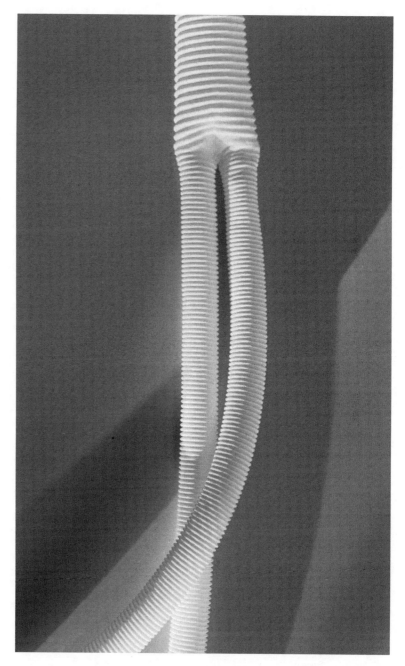

Fig 10.19 Woven artificial aorta developed by Culzean Textile Solutions

11

Cast Metal

Fig 11.0 Green sand for casting and pattern

Cast Metal
Arthur McLuckie and Son, Dalry

Grey iron and ductile iron are produced with a 500kW, water-cooled, 1 tonne induction furnace, which can produce a tonne of molten metal in about one hour from cold. The molten metal can reach temperatures of 1200°C. Different metal mixes are used for different types of product. Generally ductile iron is used for drain covers, gulleys and various other road castings, whereas grey iron is used for the engineering castings, which include pulley wheels and capstans for boats. The softer grey iron allows for milling of the material after casting.

Process
Moulds are made in two halves: the cope and the drag. Moulding involves packing and compacting green sand around a pattern in a casting box,

Fig 11.1 Aluminium pattern fixed to base board

Fig 11.2 Pattern form transferred to green sand mould

Fig 11.3 Steel pattern boxes for green sand

Fig 11.4 Pattern and mould

mechanically or by hand. The drag half is then turned over forming the lower half of the mould and the pattern is then removed leaving an imprint (mould) in the sand mix. This process is then repeated to form the 'cope'. The green sand is then dried out. The process of removing the water content from the green clay-sand mix sets the sand solid. Before the cope and drag are assembled, gates are placed into the mould along with a Sprue in the cope. The sprue is where the metal is poured and the gates/gating system is the route designed for the metal to correctly flow into the mould. These paths into the mould set solid during fabrication and are known as runners. With road castings, the two pieces of the mould are held together with a number of 25kg weights, while with engineering castings, the two halves of the mould are mechanically fixed to prevent the cope 'floating' during the pouring of the molten metal.

Fig 11.5 Green sand mould for small surface boxes

Fig 11.6 Compacting green sand into the moulds

Fig 11.7 Green sand moulds drying out

Fig 11.8 Resin-bonded sand mixer

Green Sand

Green sand is a clay-bonded sand being a mixture of silica, clay and water. It is the water content which affects its consistency and water is regularly added to achieve the right mix. Green sand is compacted by hand around a pattern (of timber or aluminium) in a casting box. Green sand is widely used in the production of heavy castings as it is easy to use and inexpensive. It can be endlessly recycled, albeit with some additives such as bentonite (a water absorbing clay).

Resin-Bonded Sand

Resin-bonded sand is used specifically for engineering castings where a finer surface finish is desirable. The addition of an epoxy-based resin means that the sand sets solid; however, a Richards reclamation plant is able to recycle the resin-impregnated sand as fast as it is produced.

Fig 11.9 Compacting sand into the mould

Fig 11.10 Detail of manhole cover mould

Fig 11.11 Steel casting boxes for resin-bonded sand

Fig 11.12 Sealing resin-bonded sand

Patterns

Patterns are the mould-forming tool with the mould cavity being made from the pattern. They can be made from many materials including metals, timber, plastics or plaster. Pattern making is an art in itself and requires a different set of tools and disciplines; many foundries do have a pattern shop or at least access to a good pattern maker. The development of CNC (Computer Numerically Controlled) milling has affected the speed and cost of producing new patterns, but has yet to seriously affect the processes of iron founders, some of whose patterns can be over a hundred years old.

Fig 11.13 Burning off the sealing compound

Fig 11.14 Thermal sleeves used in the moulds

Fig 11.15 Mould ready for molten metal with casting tube and two thermal sleeves

Fig 11.16 Buckets for transferring molten metal to moulds

Ductile Iron

Ductile iron is a development of cast iron. The problems with cast iron was that it was a brittle, non-malleable iron-carbon alloy. In 1942, the metallurgical engineer Keith D. Millis discovered that when adding a copper alloy into the iron mix, spheroidal graphite nodules formed, which increased the tensile strength of the material and introduced ductility (malleability).

Metal Mixes

Metal mixes are adjusted to produce either grey iron or ductile iron of different grades in accordance with British and European standards. Mixes include:

Pig iron - raw iron from furnace-smelted iron ore
Returns - scrap from previous castings
Scrap steel - from scrap dealers
Carbon (in a graphite pellet form)
Silicon (in aggregate form)

Fig 11.17 Pig iron used as part of the ductile mix

Fig 11.18 Detail of furnace with scrap being melted down

Fig 11.19 The induction furnace

Fig 11.20 The test pot measures carbon/silicon content

Each batch of metal is tested using a testing pot, (see Fig 11.20) which digitally measures carbon and silicon content and is used to monitor quality for certified products (ISO:9000 and British Standard certified). These measurements also record the foundry's carbon emissions, which are tested yearly in accordance with UK and European Directives.

Ladles

Foundries use a number of ladles for transferring the molten material to the moulds. For smaller jobs, when a large amount of material is not required, two-man, hand ladles are used. For larger jobs, a crane ladle is used. This can carry up to 1 tonne of molten material and is mounted on a gantry crane. The ladle is rotated or tipped using a geared hand-wheel, and as a lip-pouring ladle it must be skimmed before pouring to prevent impurities such as dross or slag entering the mould (see Fig 11.23).

Fig 11.21 Furnace being hydraulically lifted

Fig 11.22 Molten metal reaches a temperature of 1200°C

Fig 11.23 Crust or slag is removed by skimming before the metal is poured

Fig 11.24 Pouring the metal

Finishing

Once the metal has set, finishing or surface cleaning requires the removal of the gates and risers. The castings are then usually cleaned using a shotblasting process where they are bombarded with small abrasive metal shot to create a smooth surface finish. This happens in a blasting cabinet with a rotating internal platform so that all sides of the casting are cleaned. Some of the grey iron castings are machined after fabrication for a smoother finish and finer dimensional tolerance.

Fig 11.25 Cast cutting wheels

Fig 11.26 Cast pulley wheels

Fig 11.27 Arthur McLuckie pouring the metal

Fig 11.28 Patterns for bench-end pieces

The Fabricator
Arthur McLuckie & Son was founded in 1967 as a specialist producer of road castings. They have developed to produce products including ornamental iron-work and engineering castings. They are a family firm with Arthur and Johnnie running the engineering castings/road castings respectively and sister and aunt based on-site in the head office. They have pattern making facilities and a shotblasting plant on site.

Fig 11.29 Shotblasting unit for cleaning the castings

Fig 11.30 Mould and timber pattern for wheel

Fig 11.31 Cast gulley covers

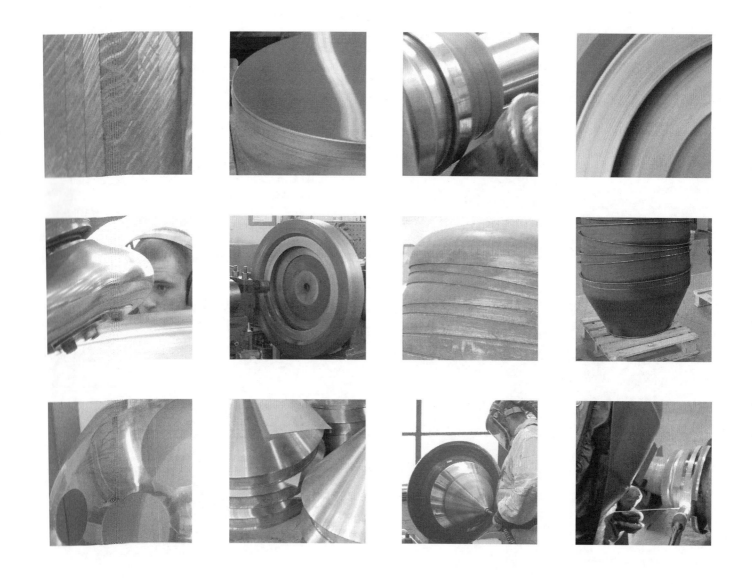

12

Spun Metal

Fig 12.0 Stainless steel

Spun Metal
Metal Spinners Group, Newcastle-upon-Tyne

Metal Spinning
Metal spinning is the forming of flat circular sheets of metal around a mandrel to create three-dimensional, rotationally symmetrical, profiled products. Metal spinning has been traced back as far as ancient Egypt.

The Material
Sheet materials such as carbon steel and aluminium are cut into circular blanks ready for spinning. The circular blanks can also have their centre removed forming rings, which can also be spun. Most metals can be spun, including stainless steel and alloys such as Titanium and Hastelloy, in sizes up to 4.25m diameter and 40mm thick. With some metals, such as stainless steel, heat is

Fig 12.1 Discs cut and ready for spinning

Fig 12.2 Machine for cutting discs from metal sheets

Fig 12.3 Spinning shapes by hand with profiled tools

Fig 12.4 Automated metal spinning of aluminium rings

directly applied to the metal using a large gas powered blowtorch during the spinning process to increase its ductility and prevent cracking.

The Process

Using a controllable, rotary machine similar to a lathe, a circular, flat blank is clamped between the mandrel (pattern) and tailstock. As the metal is rotated at speeds up to 600rpm, spinning rollers are applied to the sheet metal to wrap it around the mandrel. Depending on the size and thickness of the sheet metal, the rollers are either applied by hand or with the help of hydraulic power. There are two types of process, which can be described as metal spinning: one is spinning which uses both tensile and compressive forces to plasticise the metal, and the other is flow forming which uses a purely compressive force. The spinning process will produce a varying wall thickness in order to take the

Fig 12.5 Automated metal spinning: detail of tool

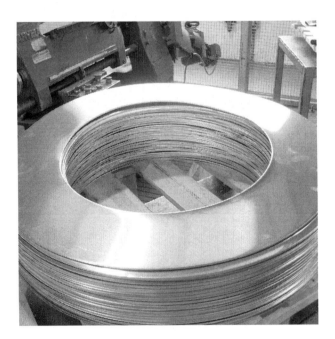

Fig 12.6 Aluminium rings ready for spinning

Fig 12.7 Patterns and mandrels for differently profiled spinnings

Fig 12.8 Spinning process in progress

shape of the mandrel, whereas flow forming uses special rollers to maintain a consistent and controlled sheet thickness reduction throughout the product. Flow forming is used for the production shapes and represents a significant technological development in the field.

The Mandrel

The mandrels or patterns for small, hand-spun products were originally made from wood. Now, however, various grades of iron and tool steel are used: the mandrels are milled on-site for each job, and stored for reuse (see Fig 12.7). The geometry of the mandrel will determine the spinning time, with sharp ridges taking longer so as not to crack the metal. Re-tooling for spinning remains relatively inexpensive as it is only the mandrel (pattern), that needs to be fabricated or remilled from an existing mandrel pattern.

Fig 12.9 This machine is working at 600rpm

Fig 12.10 This machine spins and mills the metal surface

Fig 12.11 Spinning and forming profiled aluminium rings

Fig 12.12 'Dished ends' for storage tanks and silos.

CNC and PNC

As the process of spinning and flow forming becomes more automated, CNC (Computer Numerical Control) is increasingly used to regulate the fabrication process. Used in conjunction with PNC (Playback Numerical Control) the skill of the machine operator is recorded as a toolpath and subsequently refined as a set of digital repeatable commands to optimise the automation process.

Dimensional Accuracy

Dimensional accuracy is important for many of the spun products. The components are checked by hand and with portable Coordinate Measurement Machines (CMM). CMM use an articulated arm fixed to a base plate in order to data-log a series of coordinates across the surface of a component. The portable CMM device allows dimensions to be checked without removing parts from the tooling.

Fig 12.13 Spun drums for concrete mixers

Fig 12.14 Spinning a large cylindrical component

Fig 12.15 Component for medical scanning machine. Extremely high dimensional tolerances are required

Fig 12.16 Tool heads are different for each job

Products

While most spinning work is bespoke, in so much as each job requires a different mandrel, there are certain standard products that are traditionally formed by spinning, e.g. dished ends for boilers and other bulk handling containers, as well as cones and hemispheres for the air handling, and the food and chemical processing industries.

Fig 12.17 Water-jet cutting of stainless steel

Fig 12.18 A spun component with 'water-jet' cut openings

Fig 12.19 These highly automated processes still require the eye and judgement of the operator

Fig 12.20 Highly polished container lids with welded top

The Fabricator

The Metal Spinners Group was formed in 1953. In 1997 a management buy-in established the current company structure, which operates out of two sites in Newcastle-upon-Tyne and with over 40 machines offers the largest range of spinning processes in Europe. The Metal Spinners Group also specialise in added value spun products, which include profiling, welding and polishing. Welding processes include TIG (Tungsten Inert Gas welding - see Fig 12.21) and MIG (Metal Inert Gas welding). Profiling processes include water-jet, plasma and laser cutting (see Fig 12.17). High quality polished finishes from course ground to bright polish are also achievable (see Fig 12.22).

Fig 12.21 'Value added' finishing fabrication work

Fig 12.22 Polishing conical components

Fig 12.23 Factory floor with MRI scanner components shown in the right of the picture

Glossary of Processes

In compiling this glossary, the authors have, in certain cases, adapted various dictionary definitions. This is because (a) the generic terms are not necessarily specific to the word's use in the context of fabrication, and (b) where it is specific, definitions rely upon describing the complete task, e.g. carve would refer to the shaping of wood or stone, telling you nothing about the tool or actions.

Bend: To cause or to assume a curved shape by bringing material into a state of tension.

Carve: To make a shape by an eroding action usually by applying the force of a cutting or abrasive tool.

Cast: The act of pouring a fluid or plastic substance into a mould, where the material solidifies through a chemical 'state' change.

Cut: The application of any tool whose impact on a material will cause linear penetration, usually to separate the material into parts.

Fair: To make a surface smooth and flowing by the acts of abrasion and polishing.

Fold: To bend a material along a fixed linear axis.

Grind: To reduce a material to small particles by pounding or abrading with a harder material.

Laminate: To bond two or more sheets of material in layers to form a thicker sheet.

Mill: To process raw materials using machinery that grinds and pulverises by employing a rotary motion.

Plane: To shave fine layers off the surface of a material - traditionally wood - with a cutting blade, with the intention to smooth or shape that material.

Roll: To shape or 'spread' a material by using the pressure of rolling a tube over its surface.

Route: To remove a channel from the surface of a material through the action of a rotary cutting tool.

Saw: The application of various tools, having a thin blade or disk with a toothed edge for the cutting of materials.

Spin: To form a sheet metal by rotating it and fabricating a rotationally symmetrical deformation around a mandrel.

Stitch: To fasten or join together with a single in-and-out movement of a threaded needle.

Turn: To give a rounded form to a material by rotating against a cutting tool.

Weave: To construct a surface by interlacing strips or strands of material.

Weld: To join (metals and plastics) by applying heat, either with pressure or with an intermediate or filler material with a high melting point.

Wind: To turn completely or repeatedly so as to become coiled about anything.

Company Information

1 John Dent Engineering
1432a Clock Tower Road, Isleworth,
Middlesex,TW7 6DT
Tel: +44 (0) 20 8560 4414
info@johndentengineering.com

2 Freeland Yacht Spars Ltd. (Collars)
Unit 2, Queenford Farm, Oxon. OX10 7PH
Tel. +44 (0) 1865 341 277
info@yachtspars.com
www.collars.co.uk

3 GRP Solutions
Unit B1-B2, 46 Holton Road, Holton Heath Trading
Park, Poole, BH16 6LT
Tel: +44 (0) 1202 620138
grpsolutions@btopenworld.com

4 Ormiston Wire Company
1 Fleming Way, Worton Road, Isleworth, TW7 6EU
Tel: +44 (0) 20 8569 8020
info@ormiston-wire.co.uk
www.ormiston-wire.co.uk

5 Simon Veglio (Metalwork Services)
Unit 13, Wandle Technology Park, Mill Green Road,
Mitcham, Surrey, CR4 4H
Tel: +44 (0) 7944 035586

5 The Angle Ring Company
Bloomfield Road, Tipton, DY4 9EH
Tel: +44 (0) 121 557 7241, Fax: 0121 522 4555
www.anglering.com

6 D & P Lovell Quarry Ltd
Downs Quarry, Kingston Road, Langton Matravers,
Swanage, Dorset, BH19 3JP
Tel: +44 (0) 1929 439436/439255

7 Pallam Precast
41 Lockfield Avenue, Enfield, EN3
Tel: +44 (0) 20 8805 6811
info@qualitymarble.co.uk
www.quality-marble.co.uk

8 Lindstrand Technologies Ltd
Maesbury Road, Mile Oak Industrial Estate,
Oswestry, Shropshire, SY10 8HA
Tel: +44 (0) 1691 671888
keith@lindstrandtech.com
www.inflatable-buildings.com

9 Fusion Glass Design Ltd
365 Clapham Road, London, SW9 9BT,
Tel: +44 (0) 20 7738 5888
info@fusionglass.co.uk
www.fusionglass.co.uk

10 Culzean Textile Solutions Ltd
Belford Mills, Lawson Street,
Kilmarnock, KA1 3HZ
Tel: +44 (0) 1563 549066
enquiries@culzeanfabrics.com
www.culzeanfabrics.com

11 Arthur McLuckie & Son Ltd
Carsehead Foundry, Dalry,
Ayrshire, KA24 4HZ
Tel: + 44 (0) 1294 832686
johnny@arthurmcluckie.com
www.arthurmcluckie.com

12 Metal Spinners Group Ltd
Newburn, Newcastle-upon-Tyne, NE15 9RT
Tel: +44 (0) 191 267 1011
sales@metal-spinners.co.uk
www.metal-spinners.co.uk

Sources

General:
Ashby, M. & Johnson, K. (2001). Materials and Design, The Art and Science of Material Selection in Product Design, Butterworth Heinemann.
Callicot, N. (2001). Computer-Aided Manufacture in Architecture, Architectural Press, Elsevier.
Lefteri, C., Materials for Inspirational Design, (series includes Plastic, Glass and Wood) RotoVision.
Matthews, C. (2004). Engineers' Data Book, Professional Engineering Publishing.
Strandh, S. (2004). A History of the Machine, Arrow.
Sulzer, P. (2005). Jean Prouve, Complete Works, Vols 1, 2 & 3, Birkhauser.

Preface:
Bryson, B. (2003). A Brief History of Nearly Everything, Doubleday.

Chapter 1
Stacey, M. (2001). Component Design, Architectural Press, Elsevier.

Chapter 2
Freeland, J. (2002). Collars: A Catalogue, Freeland Yacht Spars Ltd.

Chapter 3
Lootsma, B. (1998). Atelier van Lieshout: A Manual, Museum Boymans van Beunigen.

Chapter 4
www.inventionfactory.com/history/RHAwire/

Chapter 5
The ABC of Bending (2002). The AngleRing Co. Ltd.
Buyers Guide - Edition 6 (2001). ASD Klöckner
Cobb, F. (2004). Structural Engineers Pocket Book, Elsevier
www.steelbiz.org

Chapter 6
Viney, T. (2000) Purbeck Limestone: - History of Purbeck Stone, Tony Viney Workshop.

Chapter 7
National Federation of Terrazzo, Marble & Mosaic Specialists.
www.nftmms.co.uk

Chapter 8
Herzog, T. (1976). Pneumatic Structures: A Handbook of Inflatable Architecture, Oxford University. Press.
Department ot the Environment, Cedric Price, Frank Newby et al (1971). Air Structures: A Survey HMSO

Chapter 9
Lefteri, C. (2002). Glass: Materials for Inspirational Design, RotoVision.
www.britglass.org.uk

Chapter 10
Mathews, A., Hardingham M. (1994). Medical and Hygiene Textile Production - A Handbook, Intermediate Technology Publications.
Newton, N. (1993). Fabric Manufacture: A Handbook, Intermediate Technology Publications.

Chapter 11
Heine, R.W. (1967) Principles of Metal Casting, AmericanFoundrymen's Society , McGraw-Hill.
Burn, T.A. (1986). Foundrymans Handbook, Elsevier.

Chapter 12
(1975). Metal Spinning, Book 1, American Metal Spinning Association AMSA.
www.metal-spinners.net

Acknowledgments

The authors have been privileged to meet and be educated by many knowledgable individuals, from owners and managers to shopfloor workers. We sincerely hope that their patience is rewarded and that insights generously given into the practice of their various arts have been retained in some fashion within the pages of this book. Special thanks to Jeremy Freeland at Collars, John Rawling at GRP, Paul Lovell, James Carcass at Fusion, Paul Middleton at Angle Ring, Matt Ogden at Culzean, Michael Lloyd at the Metal Spinners Group, Mark Dent, Johnnie and Arthur McLuckie, Tony Viney, Lee Barnfield at Lindstrand Technologies, Mark Ormiston, and Vic Menozzi at Pallam Precast.

Authors

Pete Silver is an architect with first-hand experience of the construction industry, public sector housing, research, teaching and private practice. He has worked as a housing manager, bricklayer, clerk of works and private contractor, and completed four years as a research assistant in the Land Use Research Unit at King's College London. He has taught at the Architectural Association School of Architecture, the London College of Printing, the Bartlett School of Architecture (University College London), and at the University of Westminster School of Architecture and the Built Environment where he is currently (with William McLean) joint coordinator of Technical Studies. He has had work published in a variety of fields, and is a director of the Chartered Practice Architects (CPA) Ltd.

William McLean trained as an architect at the Architectural Association School of Architecture; he has worked in practice and taught at the Bartlett School of Architecture (University College London), and at the University of Westminster School of Architecture and the Built Environment where he is currently (with Pete Silver) joint coordinator of Technical Studies. He is working in collaboration with artist Bruce McLean and North Ayrshire Council on a project entitled Primary Space which looks at the design of primary schools. A new school in Dalry is due for completion in 2006. McLean writes a regular technical column for Architectural Design Magazine entitled McLean's Nuggets.

Simon Veglio apprenticed as a steel fabricator and went on to form his own specialist steel fabrication business. He has worked on large scale commissions with artist Bruce McLean, photographer Alastair Thain and architects such as Nigel Coates and Pierre D'Avoine. His workshop/studio is currently based in Mitcham.

Index